D0946383

Martina Navratilova

By
Jane Mersky Leder

Edited By
Dr. Howard Schroeder
Professor in Reading and Language Arts
Dept. of Elementary Education
Mankato State University

Produced & Designed By

Baker Street Productions, Ltd.

CRESTWOOD HOUSE
Mankato, Minnesota
U.S.A.

LIBRARY OF CONGRESS CATALOGING IN PUBLICATION DATA

Leder, Jane Mersky.
 Martina Navratilova.

 SUMMARY: A biography of the tennis player, originally from Czechoslovakia, who
was ranked as the top woman tennis player in the world in 1978, 1979, 1982, and 1983,
and has become the highest-paid woman athlete in history.
 1. Navratilova, Martina, 1956-   —Juvenile literature. 2. Tennis players—United
States—Biography—Juvenile literature. [1. Navratilova, Martina, 1956-   . 2. Tennis
players.] I. Schroeder, Howard. II. Title.
 GV994.N38L43   1985   796.342'092'4   [B]   [92]   84-9550
 ISBN 0-89686-252-6

International Standard Book Number: 0-89686-252-6	Library of Congress Catalog Card Number: 84-9550

PHOTO CREDITS

Cover: United Press
Sports Illustrated: (George Tiedemann) 4, 47; (Manny Millan) 5;
   (Walter Iooss, Jr.) 28, 36, 40, 41
Wide World Photos: 6, 14, 19, 20, 22-23, 24-25, 29, 33, 42-43
United Press: 11, 30, 31, 38
Focus on Sports: 44, 45

Hwy. 66 South, Box 3427
Mankato, MN 56002-3427

TABLE OF CONTENTS

Martina Navratilova moves like a tiger on the court.

INTRODUCTION

She bounds around the tennis court like a tiger, running faster than most of her opponents. Her serve is fast, too. It has been clocked at ninety miles per hour. She has won every major women's title. Martina Navratilova has earned her place as the No. 1 women's tennis player in the world.

Martina is one of the most interesting people in modern sports. She can be very demanding, and very proud. She is also funny. And those who know her say she is very

Martina shows her feelings.

thoughtful. One thing never changes—Martina shows her feelings on the tennis court.

Sometimes Martina makes a funny face when an opponent wins a point. Sometimes she throws her racket down. Such actions have caused a few people to call her a brat. Martina disagrees. "If you make a face or throw your racket down," she said, "people think you're not giving your opponent credit for a good shot. People don't realize how much the game is in your head. They don't realize that your emotions are directed at yourself, not the other player."

Martina has won more prize money than any other female athlete.

There is very little Martina can't do on the tennis court. Her earnings prove it. She has won more money than any other female athlete. By the end of the 1983 season, her career prize money totaled $6,404,589. "If I'm on, nobody can beat me," she said. "If I'm off, I beat myself."

Martina was born on October 18, 1956, in Prague, Czechoslovakia. Her family lived at a skiing center in the Krkonose Mountains. All winter long the slopes around her home glistened with snow.

Martina's parents loved to ski. So Martina started skiing soon after she learned to walk. Right from the beginning, she was good. Martina showed real promise of being a great skier.

When she was three, Martina's parents were divorced. She seldom saw her father after that. "He wasn't a real family man, and he was very emotional," she said. Her father died when she was nine years old. Years later she learned that he had killed himself.

Martina was an outgoing child. She talked easily to other children and even to adults. When she was four, Martina introduced her mother to a man whose job was fixing up tennis courts. His name was Mirek Navratti. Two years later, Mirek married Martina's mother. He became Martina's stepfather. "If he had a dollar for every hour he spent with me," said Martina, "my stepfather would be a millionaire. He loved me so much." Mirek had a motorcycle. When it snowed he would tie a rope to it and pull Martina on skis through the town.

In 1961, when Martina was five, the family moved to

Revnice. Revnice was a town of only five thousand people. Here, with less snow in the winter and few steep slopes, skiing was not very good. So Martina's parents began playing tennis at a local tennis club. They were at the courts often. They always took Martina with them. Martina had an old racket that her stepfather had shortened for her. She would hit the ball against a wall for hours.

No one was surprised at Martina's talent. Her grandmother, Agnes Semanska, had once been the second-best woman tennis player in Czechoslovakia. And Martina's parents were already well-known for their play. Tennis was the big interest in the family.

Martina thinks she was blessed. Somehow, she was better at sports than other kids. It was easy for her to run fast and jump far. She started playing tennis all the time. And she was good. "I never had to be pushed," she said. "I loved the game, especially at the net. Even as a little kid, I'd totter up to the net."

GETTING SERIOUS ABOUT TENNIS

When she was eight years old, Martina went to another town to play in her first tennis tournament. Her stepfather was so sure she would lose early in the tournament that he did not bring extra money for meals. And the officials did not want her to play. They thought she wasn't strong enough. She proved everyone wrong and made it to the semifinals. By that time, she and her stepfather were eating potatoes and cheese for every meal. They could not afford to buy anything else. Luckily, Martina's mother realized the problem and came to the tournament with more food.

When she was nine, Martina was being coached by George Parma. George was a well-known tennis player around the world. He was also an excellent coach. Martina had to take the train sixteen miles to Prague every day to practice with him. She jokes that she first got into shape by running to catch the train to Prague. Her life was very busy. She was either in school or practicing tennis.

COMMUNISM IN CZECHOSLOVAKIA

Two important events took place in 1968, when Martina was eleven. First, her coach, George Parma, left Czechoslovakia to coach in Austria. Martina's stepfather took over George's job. Second, Russia invaded Czechoslovakia. Martina was in the town of Pilsen to play in a junior tournament. She was awakened early in the morning the day the Russians invaded. She was told not to go outside. There were army tanks in the street. "There were hundreds of cars and tanks and soldiers," said Martina. "It was unreal." The tournament was canceled.

When she was thirteen, Martina played at a tournament in West Germany. When she recrossed the border to come home, she began to notice how sad people really were. The Communist government was very strict. People couldn't say, write, or even read what they wanted. Even getting a new pair of shoes was very hard. People had to wait in line for potatoes. They had to sneak extra money to the butcher to get good meat.

Despite her growing unhappiness, Martina continued to improve as a tennis player. She won her first national title in the 14-and-under division when she was fourteen. Her victory made headlines throughout Czechoslovakia. Sports fans began talking about the left-hander from Revnice as a tennis star of the future. Two years later, she won the first of three Czechoslovakian National Women's Championships.

Martina played soccer and ice hockey with boys when she wasn't playing tennis. She went to school like everyone else. "I was the third best student in my class, but I never studied," she said. "By the time I was fifteen, I didn't have time to study anyway." Martina was now playing in tournaments all over Europe and North America.

But her unhappiness with the Czech government increased with every trip she made. Coming home became sadder and sadder. Because Martina was now a well-known athlete in Czechoslovakia, the heads of the government wanted her to ask young people to join the Communist party. Martina did not want to do that. She did not like what the government had done to her country.

Martina was a well-known athlete in Czechoslovakia.

LOVE AFFAIR WITH THE UNITED STATES

In 1973, Martina made her first trip to the United States. She had never been in a country with so much to buy and eat. Martina ate everything in sight. She gained twenty pounds in just two weeks. She also bought a lot of jewelry. When she returned home, some Czechs thought Martina had enjoyed America too much. They saw that she had gained weight, and that she wore a lot of jewelry.

Although Martina was not entirely pleased with her record for 1974, it was very good for an eighteen-year-old. She had been a quarter-finalist at the French Open. She had been a finalist at the German and Italian Championships. Martina had also won a Virginia Slims tournament in the United States.

Martina's record was so good that TENNIS, a monthly tennis magazine, named Martina rookie of the year for 1974. In addition, Martina was ranked tenth in the world.

In 1975, Martina was a finalist in the Australian, French, and Italian Opens. She also made it to the finals of the Virginia Slims Championship. Martina played at the famous Wimbledon tournament in England for the first time in 1975, too. She played well for a young player and made it to the quarterfinals.

After the Wimbledon tournament, Martina and her family took a short trip to France. They returned to Czechoslovakia by car. Their route took them through Pilsen, Czechoslovakia where the Czech tennis championships were being played. Everybody at the tournament was surprised to see Martina and her family. They believed the rumors spread by some people in the government that the whole family had left the country for good.

It was after the Czechoslovakian Championships that the real trouble began. Czech officials told Martina she could not go to the United States later that summer to play in the U.S. Open. The officials said that Martina liked the United States too much. They said she was acting more and more like an American and less like a Czech. Martina dressed like an American teenager. She loved American food and music. This led to bad feelings on the part of the Czech officials.

After many talks, government officials finally changed their minds and allowed Martina to play in the U.S. Open. Martina left for the United States, leaving her family behind. Hours after losing a semifinals match to Chris Evert, Martina applied for political asylum. She asked the American government to let her stay in the United States. "I was a wreck," said Martina. "But once I was here, I knew I wasn't going to go back."

Martina was allowed to stay in the United States. She was given what is called permanent-resident status. She could live in this country, but she was not a citizen. In fact, it took six long years before she became a U.S. citizen. That bothered Martina. It was very depressing not belonging anywhere. She was a young woman without a country.

After defecting, Martina signed a contract with the Cleveland Nets of World Team Tennis. The Nets' owner, Joe Zingale, surprised her with a special gift.

14

JOYOUS FREEDOM: TERRIBLE TENNIS

After Martina left Czechoslovakia she settled in Beverly Hills, California. She spent a lot of time shopping, eating, and relaxing around a swimming pool. "It was the first time in my life when I didn't have to get permission to do anything. It all hit me at once. I went wild." Martina ate pizza and hamburgers—food she didn't have in Czechoslovakia. She was unable to lose the weight she had gained. She also went on buying sprees, spending a lot of money on gold jewelry.

Martina had a good time, but she wasn't really happy. Her family and friends were still in Czechoslovakia. She was very lonely and hated leaving her family behind. She was afraid her father would never get promoted in his job because she had defected. Martina knew that her half-sister, Jana, could not play in certain tennis clubs.

The extra weight Martina was carrying slowed her down on the tennis court. "All the freedom almost killed my tennis," she said. She thought she could rely on talent rather than hard work. She did not practice very much and did not play well. She failed to win a single tournament during an eleven-month period after moving to the United States. Her game was in big trouble.

Martina's most shocking upset came at the 1976 U.S. Open Tennis Tournament. It was the opening round. Martina was a heavy favorite to defeat her opponent, Janet Newberry. Janet was a newcomer in tennis. Almost no one had heard of her. Martina won the first set. Then she began to crumble. The second set was tied four-all when Newberry took control. Martina lost the last two sets.

The crowd was silent. There was no applause. Just an audience staring at Martina. Newberry ran over to Martina. She put her arms around her and led her off the court.

Martina was so unhappy about her loss that she sat down at courtside and cried. Reporters flocked around Martina after her loss. They tried to get her to admit that she lost because she was overweight and didn't practice much. The next afternoon, Martina announced she was taking a rest from tennis. "I was losing matches and I didn't like myself," she explained. "I was confused. I started doubting myself on everything." At the end of 1974, Martina had been a nobody in the world of tennis. Then, all of a sudden, she had become one of the top players in the world. Things happened too quickly. Martina was not ready for the pressure.

SANDY HAYNIE: MARTINA'S AGENT

Luckily for Martina, she met Sandy Haynie in the summer of 1976. Sandy is a professional golfer who had won the U.S. Open in 1974. She became Martina's agent and best friend. Sandy knew that Martina was very talented. But she also knew that Martina needed help. Martina had had a miserable year in 1976. Every athlete goes through a bad year once in awhile. But Martina had never had one before. She had a lot of trouble dealing with losing. So Sandy and Martina decided to work together. Martina moved to Dallas, Texas to be near Sandy.

The two women began working on Martina's mental attitude. One reason Martina was losing was because she let her emotions get the best of her on the tennis court. She got angry at herself for making a bad play. She let her anger affect too much of her game. Sandy helped Martina control her emotions, and also taught Martina how to relax.

Next, Sandy worked on Martina's practice habits. Martina started practicing more often. She began to see that talent was not enough. All professional athletes had talent. The best athletes practiced long and hard. If Martina was going to win, she had to do the same.

Finally, Sandy worked on Martina's eating habits. She showed Martina why she was unable to lose weight. Martina was eating too much "junk" food. She still loved American hamburgers and ice cream sodas. Martina's new diet limited the amount of "junk" food she could eat. It included more healthy foods like fish, fruit, and vegetables.

Sandy's help began to pay off. Martina started to play a few tennis tournaments again in 1977. Her game was not as good as it had been two years before, but Martina was winning often. When she did lose, she did not let her emotions get the best of her. She played steady tennis.

After awhile, Sandy no longer had the time to be Martina's agent. They are still good friends, though, and see each other as often as they can.

HARD WORK PAYS OFF

By 1978, Martina was back in top form. Her improved practice and eating habits paid off. She won seven straight tournaments on the Virginia Slims Tour and was crowned champion. She also won the French Open. But Martina's biggest win was at Wimbledon. She beat Chris Evert, her most difficult opponent. Martina was now the No. 1 women's tennis player in the world.

Martina had wanted to win Wimbledon since she was seven years old. That is when she first saw the tournament on TV. Now her dream had come true. Martina and Chris were waiting for the Duchess of Kent to present the trophies after the match.

Chris asked Martina, "How come you're not crying?"

"I am," said Martina, "but I'm trying not to show it." Martina was very happy that she had won. But she was also sad that she could not share her win with her family. The Czechoslovakian Government would not allow them to go to Wimbledon to see Martina play. Martina's family had to watch the tournament on television.

In the finals against Chris Evert-Lloyd, Martina
sweeps across court to win at Wimbledon.

Martina holds the 1978 Wimbledon trophy.

FAMILY REUNIONS

Martina continued winning in 1979. She was ranked No. 1 for the second year in a row. She again won at Wimbledon. This time her mother was there to watch her. As Martina was introduced to the crowd, her mother was crying.

Martina had been very nervous when she went to meet her mother before the match. She was silent when she first saw her. Then both of them started crying. After awhile, they were talking nonstop.

Few people knew Martina's mother would be seeing her daughter for the first time in almost four years. Martina did not tell people because she did not want news reporters around. She wanted time alone with her mother. They had a lot of catching up to do.

Later that year, Martina's parents and half sister, Jana, were allowed to come to the United States to live. They wanted to be with Martina and share the "good life" in America. Martina had bought her family a house of their own near her home in Dallas. But her family was not happy about it. They felt Martina should have had them move in with her.

None of Martina's family spoke English. That meant that they had to rely completely on Martina. That was difficult for everyone. Martina's stepfather was used to being the center of attention. Now he couldn't even speak the language.

After a short time, Martina's family returned to Czechoslovakia. Martina was disappointed that things did

In 1979, Martina and her family were reunited in Dallas, Texas.

1979 was another good year,
as Martina again won at Wimbledon.

24

not work out. She felt, however, that the decision was better for everyone. She knew that moving to a new country, learning another language, and adjusting to a different culture was very hard. Her family felt more comfortable in Czechoslovakia than they did in the United States.

THE UPS AND DOWNS OF TENNIS

Martina's tennis fell apart again in the middle of 1980. She began losing matches. Martina was not practicing more than ninety minutes every day. Sometimes she did not even practice that much. "I just hit the ball in my head some days," she said. Martina dropped from the No. 1 to the No. 3 player in the world. That is not bad for most tennis players. But it was not good enough for Martina.

Martina went on a buying spree to make herself feel better. This time she bought cars. There were seven cars in all—one for each day of the week. She bought a Pontiac, a Toyota, a BMW, a Mercedes, a Porsche, and two Rolls-Royces. But the fancy cars didn't really make her happy. She still was not winning tennis tournaments.

Then something happened that changed Martina's life. She was playing in the 1981 French Open. One evening, she met Nancy Lieberman. Nancy was in France to lead a basketball clinic. She had been the best player in women's professional basketball in the United States until the league folded in 1981. When Martina and Nancy met, it was magic. They were both very interested in all sports,

26

not just tennis and basketball. "We met," said Nancy, "and all of a sudden we were talking about the Dallas Cowboys. It was great. We really hit it off."

Nancy could see that Martina needed help. She could tell that Martina did not really believe in herself. She had been drifting along. Every time Martina got ahead of an opponent, she eased up. Martina wanted to win, but did not want to make other players feel badly.

Nancy also could tell that Martina was not in top shape. She needed to train harder, to build her strength. Martina needed a push. She needed someone to force her to be the best player in the world again. Nancy wanted to help. She was hired as Martina's trainer.

Nancy told Martina that she was going to be honest with her. She was going to tell her what was wrong with her game. Most of Martina's friends were afraid to disagree with her. They were afraid of losing Martina's friendship. But Nancy did not care. "I figured I had made it through twenty-two years without her. And she had made it twenty-four years without me," said Nancy. "If we were going to be friends, we would each have to give."

Nancy put Martina on a training schedule. She practiced tennis for three hours every day. She also worked out in a gym. She ran, played basketball, and worked with weights.

Martina also hired a nutritionist named Dr. Robert Haas. Dr. Haas made up a diet for Martina. She stopped eating butter, mayonnaise, oil, sodas, and most meats. Her energy improved. Her confidence improved. Martina began to like herself and her body.

*Dr. Richards (right) and Nancy Lieberman (left)
helped Martina.*

Later in 1981, Martina hired Dr. Renee Richards to be her coach. Richards had played in the women's tennis circuit and had once been Martina's practice partner. They had known each other since 1977. Martina had not had a full-time coach for many years. She wanted somebody there who really knew the game. "I always got away with so much," said Martina. "But you can't get by anymore. The players are too good."

Dr. Richards was a great coach. She studied Martina and the other players. She saw that Martina needed to work on her serve. She taught Martina to add top spin to

*Martina's body and mind became tough
under Dr. Richard's training.*

Martina rushes to return the ball against Chris Evert-Lloyd in the finals of the 1981 Lion Cup tournament.

her backhand. Balls with top spin are harder for an opponent to hit. Richards also helped Martina change her forehand grip, and she fixed Martina's forehand volley. (A volley is made by striking the tennis ball before it touches the ground.) Martina's body and mind became tougher under Richards' direction. Richards convinced

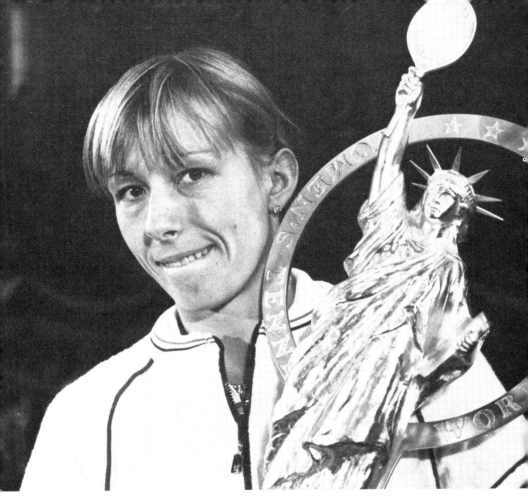

Martina beat Chris and won $100,000 for
winning first prize in the Lion Cup.

her that she did not have to make miracles to be a champion. She just had to play steady tennis, forcing her opponents to make mistakes.

By this time, Martina had won every major tournament except the U.S. Open. She wanted to win this big championship very much. It was more important than ever to win, because she had just become a U.S. citizen after six long years of waiting. Martina needed the approval of her new countrymen. She wanted to be accepted as the best American tennis player on the tour.

Martina was convinced she could win the U.S. Open this time. When she beat Chris Evert-Lloyd in the semifinals, she was just one step away from winning it all.

She played Tracy Austin in the finals and took the first set. Everything was going well. Then Martina's game fell apart. She lost the last two sets and the match. For a moment, it was the old nightmare—Martina beating herself. But something had changed. The crowd rose and gave Martina the warmest applause she had ever received. The crowd knew how much winning the U.S. Open meant to her. They knew how hard she had tried to win. The crowd appreciated her effort and wanted to show her how much they cared. Martina cupped her hands to catch her tears of joy. The people of her country were applauding her. At last she belonged. When Martina recalls that day, she is proudest of the warmth from the crowd.

1982: A SMASHING YEAR

1982 was a smashing year for Martina. She won ninety out of ninety-three matches. She finished first in fifteen out of eighteen tournaments. She was again a champion. Martina earned $1,475,055 that year. In May, she took

Martina on a television show in 1982.

over the No. 1 spot from Chris Evert-Lloyd by winning more tournaments. Her hard work had paid off. Nancy Lieberman, Dr. Richards, and Dr. Haas could not have been happier.

One of Martina's big victories in 1982 had been at the French Open in the spring. Everyone thought she would have trouble on the clay courts. But she proved them wrong. She played solid tennis. Dr. Richards' coaching was paying off.

Martina played Lisa Bonder in the second round at the French Open. She beat her badly. Yet Martina had been very nervous. After the match she talked to coach Richards.

"Why am I so nervous?" she asked Richards.

Dr. Richards just looked at her and said, "I don't know."

So before her next match at the French Open, Martina talked to herself. "This is silly," she said. "I'm an experienced woman playing kids. Enough!" Martina was fed up with worrying about winning. She settled down and won the second match against Zina Garrison. After she won, Lieberman said to her, "You were a different player out there today." Martina knew she had turned the corner.

Martina remained a changed player all the way to the finals. She beat Andrea Jaeger easily.

Then it was on to Wimbledon in England. Martina had entered as the favorite. She did not give in to the pressure. Martina had worked hard and she respected herself. She now realized that when you play your best, things work out. Each night of the tournament, Coach Richards and Martina would review ideas about the other players. They would form a game plan for the next day.

Martina had only one bad moment at Wimbledon. It did not happen on the tennis court. On the morning before the semifinals, Martina was very nervous. She could not even eat her breakfast. Lieberman told her to settle down. She reminded her not to be so sweet on the court. "You've got to stop letting up on these people," Lieberman said. "Stop feeling guilty about pounding them." Lieberman's advice worked. Martina beat Bettina Bunge in the semifinals without any problems.

Martina faced Chris Evert-Lloyd in the finals. The first

set was played in what seemed like deadly silence. Martina took the set in only twenty-two minutes. Then, Martina started falling behind. Evert-Lloyd won the second set 6-3 and was ahead in the third. But Martina had learned to deal with pressure. She went back on the attack. She was quick to the net. Her volleys and drop shots were unbeatable. The key point came when Evert-Lloyd hit an easy forehand into the net. From then on, Martina did not lose a point. She won the match easily. "I didn't let myself get into a do-or-die situation," said Martina. "In the last game, my heart wasn't even beating."

Evert-Lloyd had lost her third Wimbledon final to Martina. She was very disappointed. "I kept thinking Martina was going to crack at a certain point," said Evert-Lloyd, "but she played very well. She had to win the match. I didn't give it to her."

It had rained a lot during Wimbledon. At the Champions' Dinner held after the tournament, Martina showed her sense of humor. "Well, I'm certainly happy to be here," she told the dinner guests. "It's really been a great Wimbledon." Then she popped open a black umbrella. The guests were surprised and delighted. Martina was a great champion. And a funny one, too.

A NEW COACH

In 1983, Martina continued to do well. Her record was eighty-six wins and only one loss. She was once more on top of women's tennis.

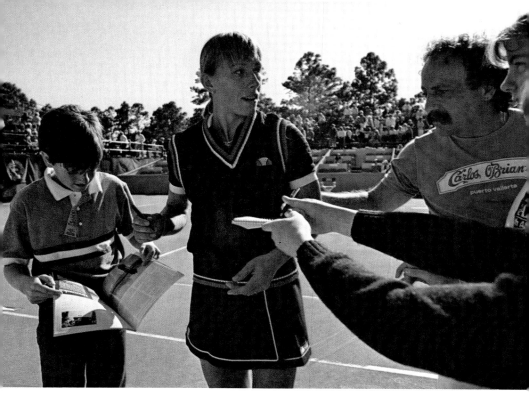

Martina signs autographs for some of her fans.

During the French Open that year, Coach Richards was not in Paris for the tournament. She was in the United States setting up her practice as an eye doctor. Martina was favored to win the French Open. She lost her only match of the year in the fourth round of the tournament. Martina was very upset about the loss.

After the French Open, Martina fired Coach Richards. She said Richards had failed to spend enough time coaching. She hinted that she lost in the French Open because Richards was not there to coach. There are those who say that Martina had already decided before the French Open to hire Mike Estep. Estep was an old friend and a professional tennis player. Whatever the reason, Dr. Richards was out.

No one denies the good effect Richards had on Martina's game. She improved Martina's self-image. She convinced Martina she could play her own game and win. The record bears out Richards' success.

Several months before the French Open, Martina had worked out with Mike Estep. Estep had reminded Martina of her strengths as an attacking player. Martina had been impressed with Estep. She finally asked him to be her new coach after the French Open. After some time, Estep agreed. His reason was simple. He felt Martina was making a bigger contribution to tennis than he was. He decided it would be an honor to work with her.

Later, at Wimbledon, Martina spent a total of 351 minutes on the court in all her matches. She lost only twenty-five games on her way to winning the tournament. At her victory party, Martina ate enough food to short-circuit her diet program for at least five weeks!

PERCENTAGE TENNIS

Mike Estep believed that Martina's volley and overhead shots were "two or three classes" better than the rest of the women. He changed her game to use those strokes. He

*Martina jumps for joy after winning her first
U.S. Open tennis championship.*

also tried to teach Martina "percentage tennis." The idea is to make the opponent hit the great shots, to make the other person play well. That's why Estep feels great players win, even when they are not playing their best. They force their opponents to make hard shots.

At the 1983 U.S. Open, Martina played perfect percentage tennis to beat Evert-Lloyd in the finals. She finally won the one tournament she had been unable to win. Martina played good, consistent tennis. She was mentally tough. There was nothing on the tennis court she could not do. "Mentally, this has to be my biggest win ever," said Martina after the match. "But when I have the game that I have now, it's easy to be mentally tough."

MARTINA TAKES THE GRAND SLAM

In 1984, Martina played Evert-Lloyd in yet another finals...the French Open. She beat Evert-Lloyd 6-3, 6-1. By winning the French Open, Martina, at age twenty-seven, had become one of only five players in tennis history to win the Grand Slam of tennis. (The Grand Slam means winning the world's four major tournaments in a row. The tournaments are Wimbledon, and the French, U.S., and Australian Opens.) Don Budge won the Grand Slam in 1938. Maureen Connolly won it in 1953. Rod Laver was a winner two times, in 1962 and 1969. Margaret Court took the Grand Slam in 1970.

In 1982, the International Tennis Federation (ITF) put

*Two of Martina's friends pose for
a group picture!*

up a $1 million bonus for any player who won the Grand Slam in a single year. Martina was the first person to collect. When the president of the ITF gave Martina the $1 million check, she quickly stuck it into her purse.

The money was just icing on the cake. Martina had now earned close to $8 million since she defected from Czechoslovakia in 1975. And she had no plans of stopping. "My next goal," she said, "is to win the Grand Slam again!"

A NEW BREED

At age twenty-seven, Martina is growing stronger every day. Her brain and muscles are checked by a computer.

Martina in the kitchen of her house.

"Martina is practically plugged into a computer at all times," explained Dr. Haas. "She will be the first example of what I think will be a new breed of athlete."

When Martina eats, she does it according to Dr. Haas' diet. When she trains, she does it with a computer. The computer suggests workouts based on the condition of Martina's body.

A computer also gives Martina information about other players. Not everyone thinks using a computer works. Jimmy Connors is one of the world's best male tennis players. He thinks "using a computer for strategy is foolish." He feels once you are out on a tennis court, you are out there by yourself.

Martina on her way to the finals of the Computerland Women's Indoor Tournament.

Winning against Evert-Lloyd in the 1984
Virginia Slims Tennis Tournament finals.

Ted Tinling, a tennis expert, feels much the same way. He does not think the "bionic woman" is always going to be the champion. He isn't sure that a computer can im-

Martina hits a backhand (left), and follows through (right).

prove a player's skill on the tennis court.

Martina does not think much about the ideas behind

using the computer. She looks at the results. "My body changed almost overnight after going on the diet. I built up muscle very quickly. Right now I am as strong as I've

ever been." Martina wants to be the best-conditioned woman on the tennis tour. She wants to win Wimbledon at forty years of age. And she wants to stay as young as she can after her tennis career ends.

Dr. Haas says that, for years, tennis players trained only by playing tennis. But, says Haas, many muscle groups are not even used when out on the tennis court. Martina, however, does exercises to use all of her muscles. She is programmed to get the most out of her body.

Martina's training program is a secret. Only she, Dr. Haas, Lieberman, and Estep know the details. Printouts from the computer are in a special code. No stranger can figure out what they say. The computer information about Martina's opponents is also top secret. "Imagine if you had the inside scoop on your biggest opponents," said Haas. "Would you want them to get their hands on it?"

For now, Martina is having fun with the program. She thinks it has made her a much better tennis player.

MARTINA'S FUTURE

Martina's goal is to win a place in tennis history as the best woman player ever. No matter what the historians decide, Martina will surely be ranked near the top. Her speed, her strokes, and her ability to move make her one of the best.

Martina does not know what she wants to do when her tennis days are over. She hopes her best years are not behind her. One thing she knows for sure. She will quit

*Martina wants to be remembered
as a champion.*

while she is at the top. "When there's no place to go but down," she said, "I don't want to be around." She wants to be remembered as a champion.

Champions are people who give their sport their best. They don't waste anything. Martina Navratilova is a true champ. She does not think she is a better person because she wins. Her pride comes from giving tennis everything she has. The world of sports treasures such dedication!

MARTINA NAVRATILOVA'S PROFESSIONAL STATISTICS

Year	Matches		World Rank	Money Earned
	W	L		
1975	88	20	3	173,668
1976	41	15	4	128,535
1977	66	15	3	300,317
1978	80	9	1	450,757
1979	90	12	1	747,548
1980	86	13	3	749,250
1981	79	11	3	865,437
1982 (singles)	90	3	1	1,338,200
1982 (doubles)	68	4	1	136,855
1983 (singles)	86	1	1	1,330,330
1983 (doubles)	61	2	1	125,700
1984 (singles)*	13	1		125,000
1984 (doubles)*	11	0		22,500
1984 Bonus Earnings*				229,100

*As of March 26, 1984 (prior to winning Grand Slam)

48